PLEBEIAN POETRY

Terrance John Cummins

WESTBOW
PRESS®
A DIVISION OF THOMAS NELSON
& ZONDERVAN

WestBow Press books may be ordered through booksellers or by contacting:

WestBow Press
A Division of Thomas Nelson & Zondervan
1663 Liberty Drive
Bloomington, IN 47403
www.westbowpress.com
1 (866) 928-1240

ISBN: 978-1-9736-5747-7 (sc)
ISBN: 978-1-9736-5746-0 (hc)
ISBN: 978-1-9736-5748-4 (e)

Library of Congress Control Number: 2019903225

Print information available on the last page.

WestBow Press rev. date: 07/19/2019

Dedicated to my friends in Ireland.
Know that I carry my love for you and for Ireland wherever I go.

Plebeian Poetry

1. Like the Rain

Like the water falling from the sky
Like breaking day and the rising sun
You're in the wind that passes by
And surely you will come

Years our fathers waited
And we waited for longer still
When it arrives we'll be elated
When your feet land on that eastern hill

You will come to us like the rain
And you'll arrive like the dawn's light
With lamb's wool and lion's mane
With servant's heart and eyes burning bright

2. Jot and Tittle

To say a lot in a little
You must shape every jot and tittle

To say a lot in a little
You must craft every piece that you whittle

3. Oh Lord

Protect me, oh, Lord
My heart from failing
And my eyes from tearing

Guard me oh Lord
My will from faltering
My soul from following
That deceptive path of ill

Cleanse me oh God
My body from sins
My mind from slipping
And my mind from unwholesome sowing

Lead me oh Lord
To the rock that is higher than I
To the land You have promised
Into your presence once more

Send me oh Lord
To the people You have chosen
With the Word you have spoken
Into your presence once more

4. Fools Like Me

Poems are for fools like me
Daydreaming about who they may be

Poems are for fools like me
Who have the luxury of being free

Poems certainly are for fools like me
Writing about what they can and can't see

For God has made all and awesome is He
But poems are left for fools like me

5. Like a Man

Some men use brick and brawn
To find a way to live on

Some add to knowledge ever increasing
To live forever, without ceasing

I wish my words would float forever
And fly through time like a feather

However, they'll pass away like a man
But God's Word will forever stand

6. The Tempest and Rain

Swallowed again by the tempest and rain
Covered continuously like a thick cloud
Torn once more by the night and pain
I'm in the pit as by darkness slain
It's crippled me and I'm entirely bowed
Swallowed again by the tempest and rain
How could I to you explain
This curse to which I'm endowed?
Torn once more by the night and pain
Like an assault and war upon my brain
How in my health could I be so proud?
Swallowed again by the tempest and rain
Shall I forever in this state remain?
Will this sickness smother me with its shroud?
Torn once more by the night and pain
Surely it seems my life so young has waned
As a mute yearning to scream aloud
Swallowed once more by the tempest and rain
Torn once more by the night and pain

7. To You I Bow

Toppled over
And climbing still
Have I surrendered
To Satan's will?
Can I return
To God's sacred hill?

Straightening out
And walking now
With thankfulness
To You I bow
Thinking clearly
But I know not how

8. Not in Man

Can a man change his ways
And be fruitful again?
Can he resist his sins?
I'm sure he can

Not in man though
This power lies
Only in Him
Who lives in the skies

9. Within the Earth

Died and buried within the earth
All men will be put to rest and lay
Covered and swaddled beneath the turf
Once filled with joy and childlike mirth
In this state we wished we stayed
Died and buried within the earth
We've been traveling here since birth
Now arrived we begin to fade
Covered and swaddled beneath the turf
What measures a life? What is its worth?
Now that our greatest debt is paid
Died and buried within the earth
Back to our fathers, where we came forth
With all those who took the blade
Covered and swaddled beneath the turf
Back to the dust, our original hearth
Time to meet thy God to whom we prayed
Died and buried within the earth
Covered and swaddled beneath the turf

Terrance John Cummins

10. Forever Stay

What if I could travel to a land
Where I'd forever stay

Oh that I had wings like a dove
And could fly away
To a land where I'd forever stay

With rivers rushing into the quay
And tides receding into the bay
In a land that I'd forever stay

I'd gladly spend and be spent
To be called or to be sent
To a land where I'd forever stay

So when my years begin to wane
And when I'm old and gray
I'll look forward to my gain
In a land where I'll forever stay

11. The Blood of His Cross

He paid the debt and met the cost
Redeeming me from sin that I never could
Having made peace by the blood of His cross
All His work it seemed but a loss
Christ sacrificed Himself for all men's good
He paid the debt and met the cost
My sins away from me He would eternally toss
Taking on shame and even death He withstood
Having made peace by the blood of His cross
Making me new and purging the dross
Bridging the divide that I never could
He paid the debt and met the cost
The straight and narrow He carried me across
His purpose only He understood
Having made peace by the blood of His cross
He bled for His enemies, the sinners and the lost
He paid the debt and met the cost
Having made peace by the blood of His cross

12. Wind or Weather

As a hen gathers her chicks
For protection under her wings
As a mother swaddles a child
And to him softly sings

As a stork nests with his family
And a fox with her pups in the ground
Christ's presence covers me
And within Him I'll be found

The Lord will ever cover me
Under His shadows and feathers
Within His hand I will be
No matter the wind or the weather

13. Drowning

The water came up to my neck
And with panic I cried
I wouldn't expect
That he would have passed me by

He walked on the waves
And over the deep
To set free Sin's slaves
And give an inheritance to the meek

He climbed in the boat
And up to the bow
The vessel still floats
And we're at the shore now

14. Prolific

I don't have high hopes
But I want to be prolific
And dreadfully specific
May my words cut to the heart
Along with the verses I exhort
Be they long or be they short

May they be a testimony
Let them glorify the One
And praise Him for all He's done

15. Invisible Hand

What is this invisible hand
Speaking forth creation out of nothing
And from the waters calling land?

What is this eternal power
That split the seas
And secures the righteous tower

It is Your Word
Spoken unto us
Of which we have heard

Plant this Word deep
Within our hearts and tongues
In our minds let it steep

His Word is truth!
His Word is light!
Remember it in your youth!

Yes, remember it day by day
Keep it inside you
Until you are old and gray

This Word won't age. No, never
Year by year it remains
This Word will live forever

16. At My Door

Sin lies at my door
And its desire is for me

With divided heart
Like waves on the shore
To stay or to depart
From the beast lying at my door

Two steps forward
Now falling backward more and more
It seems I'm slipping toward
That demon at my door!

A wretched man is all I see
How much longer can my soul endure
That gripping sin who desires me
Is still lying at my door!

17. Enigma

What an enigma this flesh holds
What lies behind these two windows
How perplexed I am by their gray folds
How puzzled by their ebbs and flows

Who can understand this mystery?
Who can perceive this paradox?
Which has plagued men throughout history
Making us a lamb instead of a fox

When will men see in clarity
Our earthly counterpart?
When will this union take parity?
We men don't know where to start

18. Gather

Come let us gather
We who were once enemies
We who were once scattered

He has made us a home
In His holy mountain
So we no longer have to roam

Meet your new family
Your brothers and sisters
With whom you'll forever be

19. The Day I Wished to Die

My mind surrendered and heart began to cry
I felt bludgeoned and I was hit
On the day I wished to die
To hope that in the grace I'd lie
The spirit within had quit
My mind surrendered and heart began to cry
So young! Yet life had passed me by
My strength had failed with my brain and wits
On the day I wished to die
How could this happen to me and why, why, why?
I felt abandoned and thrown into a pit
My mind surrendered and heart began to cry
On your wings I wished to fly
And my being within me split
On the day I wished to die
But you took me to the rock that is higher than I
And rebuilt me bit by bit
My mind surrendered and heart began to cry
On the day I wished to die

20. The Artist of Our Days

Never let your love depart
Because of it I will sing
Keep it close to my heart

This light shall endure long
It'll guide me through and through
Emboldening the weak and making me strong

Mounted up like eagles in the air
Running and not growing weary
And giving You my every care

You are the author of our story
The artist of our days
As You mold us from glory to glory
And guide us in Your ways

21. Pure as Gold

It is a nightmare and not a dream
These light and momentary afflictions
As hard as they may seem
They are which test our convictions

Though we're seeking God with earnest
And do the things we're told
We've been thrown into the furnace
But it refines us as pure as gold

Don't try and seek a buffer
Or escape by some special privilege
We've all been called to suffer
We're conforming to His image

22. This We Know

With arms spread wide
And a hole in his side

My Savior hung from the tree
And bore punishment for me

His blood streaked the road
As He bore the cross as a goad

They laid Him in the tomb
A dark, damp, earthly womb

For He rose again to show
His deity, this we know

He will soon appear in the clouds
And bring nothing to the proud

Yes, Christ will come again
But only the Father knows when

23. Youthful Adolescence

I found a treasure in a field
In my youthful adolescence
The Word which is now my shield
And leads me into His presence

I received a pearl of great price
When I was a young man
It was the message of sacrifice
Any storm I can now withstand

His Spirit became a fire
Shut up within my bones
A new consuming desire
Once I made His word my own

24. In the Depths

With the Lord wisdom is kept
Sitting forever at His feet
Deeper and deeper in the depths
Like East and West who never meet

With the Lord there is peace
Like rivers and mighty streams
Flowing to the weak and least
Giving rest and pleasant dreams

The Lord, He is love
Loving the lost and the outcast
Descending as a dove
And serving as the last

The Lord, He will come
Like the spring and winter rains
As sure as the rising sun
And the setting of the same

Terrance John Cummins

25. I Will Sing

I will sing of your grace
Even though it'll be out of tune
I long for your embrace
But you are still coming soon

I will make mention of your deeds
And proclaim your mighty works
Sowing it forth as seeds
Wherever the road may fork

I will tell of your mercies too
That are new for me each day
As the grasses are cloaked in dew
And in this mercy I will stay

26. The Race

We all have a race before us
We all have a path to find
In our God we must trust
Wherever the road may wind

He will guide us continually
And satisfy our soul in drought
Though our sins return habitually
And we harbour distrust and doubt

His hand will show us the way
And in Him we live and move
Come whatever may
He'll surely show us approved

27. Our Creator

In His faithfulness we hope
And His word will be on our tongue
Creating us that for Him we'd grope
He'll breathe life back into our lungs

He set our appointed boundaries
And the times and seasons as well
Casting us in His heavenly foundry
With boasts of these deeds I'll tell

He's commanded all men to repent
And turn back to the Greater
His judgement will not relent
If we depart from our Creator

28. Your Courts

Better is one day in your courts
Than a thousand outside of them
Your city stands as strong as a fort
And its foundations are gems

One day within it I'll dwell
With God and the Lamb as light
I'll hear the wedding bells
And there'll be no more night

I'll live forever with the Lord
And before the angels I'll stand
Because of our everlasting accord
And the blood of the lamb

Terrance John Cummins

29. Enter In

With boldness I enter in
And bow before your throne
Cleansing me from sin
I pray with an earnest groan

Let my prayers rise before you
Like incense to your nose
I'll pray your Word that's true
And watch as the Spirit goes

You bring the righteous an answer
From your heavenly mount
Even when doubt spreads like cancer
And our failings are too numerous to count

30. Like Swords

Whose words are worthy enough
To capture the majesty?
Should they be soft or tough
Or woven as a tapestry?

No speech can compare
To your faultless words
Which strips the forest bare
And separated soul and spirit like swords

Our rhetoric is feeble and fleeting
Like a rambling empty song
Our talk is shallow and without meaning
Like the clanging of a gong

31. Purest Candor

If I can speak with purest candor
And make myself clearly known
Many times I have delusions of grandeur
About the words that I have sown

A man should be humble
And not lifted up
So that he doesn't stumble
Or drink from a wrathful cup

Keep your pride in check
And your presumption keep low
To protect your own neck
From correction's fatal blow

32. Worry

Worry, worry
Oh what shall I do

Worry, worry
It's pitifully true

Worry, worry
Each obsession is bad

Worry, worry
I'm sorrowfully clad

Worry, worry
It doesn't do much

Worry, worry
I've felt its cold touch

33. Darkly Lay

I darkly lay
On this cruel bed
Trying to slay
The thoughts in my head

Repeat and repeat
The same things again
Will I ever defeat it?
Oh please tell me when

There's no telling how
This story will end
But I'll tell you right now
My brain I can't mend

You've felt this too?
You've been here before?
I never knew
It sat at your door

Rescue me please!
From this torturous pit
Bring my mind to ease
On this bed while I sit

34. My Heart it Will Ring

Words of a fool
I pen and I write
My mind as the tool
Who I usually fight

At least it brings something
To be read by someone
My hand it will ring
Like bells when they're rung

Take these sayings with you
Hide them in your heart
I'll write some more too
Before I depart

35. Double Trouble

Thinking and pondering
And worry some more
The Devil is sauntering
Right through my core

Give me some trouble
And some brokenness too
My work will just double
And it'll be read by you

36. Life Goes So Fast

I wonder and stare
At my present and past
It's truly not far
How life goes so fast

One minute we're here
And another we're gone
Our lives I fear
Are from dusk until dawn

You'll soon be erased
Like pencil on paper
To the grave we race
You are truly a vapor!

37. Mother

Mother, I love you
And forever I'll say
You felt my pain too
On my darkest of days

I'll eternally remember
Your face how it glowed
That day in November
When I packed and came home

You've been ever faithful
And in the future you'll see
I will be ever grateful
For how you loved me

38. Shepherd of My Soul

I will ever mention
The shepherd of my soul
Who relieves the tension
And fills my spirit's hole

He leads me beside a river
For His righteousness' sake
Although I may quiver
My peace He shall make

His staff protects me from foes
And he's right there by me
Through life's bitter woes

39. Alas for the Day

Alas for the day
The Day of the Lord is here
For your deeds you will pay
And judgment is near

Your reprisal shall return
And rest on your head
Your works he shall burn
In judging the living and the dead

As you yourself have done
It will so be done to you
Among men there is none
Who are righteous and true

Turn while there's time
Return to the One
Repent of your crimes
Before the day comes

40. Under a Steeple

This is for my people
All throughout the Earth
Who gather under a steeple
And celebrate new birth

The sinners become saints
The sheep of his flock
The world says we taint
And progression we block

Love not the world
Nor the things that are in it
Rejoice when you're hurled
And torn bit by bit

We're not from this place
We're sojourners and strangers
Set flint in your face
And run toward the danger

41. Break Zone

I'm stuck in the break zone
And the water is white
My voice loses tone
And my muscles are tight

It's pulling me under
And pushing me down
As I'm torn asunder
I'm beginning to drown

There's a light on the surface
And a hand reaching through
My Savior didn't miss
And I finally came to

42. Green and Gray

My heart it is breaking
As I stand on this rock
My hands they are shaking
As I shepherd my flock

The land is so green
And the skies are so gray
My face now is lean
As I starve day by day

I left my maiden behind
On a far distant shore
Our souls we did bind
Before they were torn

I can no longer bear
I'm tossing and turning
This love we did share
Is burning and burning

My love I'll come back
And end this cruel strife
We'll no longer lack
As we start this new life

43. Treasures Inside

I have these words in my being
Like treasures inside
I'm overflowing with meaning
It's too hard to hide

I've had a good streak
I'm sure I'll write more
But my poems are a tad bleak
And my rhyming is poor

44. These Thoughts That Are Raging

The war is still waging
Between the folds and valleys
My soul is now engaging

My face now is aging
From the stress that I bear
And my strength it is fading

My head that you're caging
Can no longer withstand
These thoughts that are raging

45. Trust in the Son

What's the substance of a man?
What captures his soul
If his steps he did plan
But never reached his goal?

What do we leave for others
On the day that we die?
When our last breath has been smothered
After we said our goodbyes

Will your works be forgotten
And your words will they stand
When your casket is rotten
And life's slipped through your hands?

Moss will grow thick
On the front of your grave
Your grandchildren will be sick
And die of old age

But death's not the end
It has only begun
Towards life the river bends
If you trust in the Son

46. Rivers in the South

Like rivers in the south
Your courts will endure
Your Word will be in my mouth
When I'm at the temple door

Take this humble gift
With fire it'll burn
My heart I will shift
And towards you I'll turn

Have Your Spirit go with me
From Your court I will go
You've filled me with glee
And this I fully know

47. My Words

What does it really take
To accomplish your dreams?
Your core you must shake
And give it all it would seem

I have this vision
Mutable, ductile, yet fixed
That stays with me in transition
And when life gets all mixed

My words must be heard
And captured by the masses
Let them float like a bird
And spread out like gasses

My hopes they remain
And my dreams are secure
The world wants me tame
But I'll keep dreaming some more

48. My Poems

My poems are so short
In length they are lacking
But my being they exhort
And my essence they're unpacking

I pray they find you well
That they mend you like sutures
And like a wave they would swell
On into the future

49. Out of the Darkness

Out of the darkness
In creation it burst forth
Your words in their starkness
Gave light its quick birth

It spreads to the corners
The nooks all around
When You separated the waters
And brought forth the dry ground

Today it still shines
With brilliance everywhere
Giving life of all kinds
Its beauty we all share

50. The Longings Deep Down

How much do you know
Of me and myself?
Only what I show
Like pictures on a shelf

You don't know my abyss
The longings deep down
But some things you won't miss
If you do stick around

You'll see my mistakes
And some of my flaws
But I'll never be fake
Or lie for no cause

51. This Life That We live

From water we're born
And created anew
Between these we're torn
It's sad but it's true

From dust we're created
To dust we'll return
Our justification will be stated
Or we'll be judged and be burned

That day when it arrives
Whenever it is
Will be a surprise
To end this life that we live

52. His Door

I'm climbing and climbing
Like waves on the shore
Still steadily rising
Reaching up to Your door

I'm entering Your presence
With an expectant and eager eye
I'm seeing Your essence
As Your glory abides

Boldly I enter Your gates
You've given us a place
To escape men's cruel fate
And to walk in Your grace

53. Expressing What I Mean

It keeps my cogs turning
Like a well-oiled machine
I have learned and am learning
To express what I mean

It makes me uncover
My emotions within
It has me rediscover
All the places I've been

Layer by layer I peel
My thoughts slip into words
I begin to reveal
The things that I've heard

This poetry is alive
Its beginning to seem
Into its river I dive
From the bridge's high beams

54. For One and For All

My lines may be terse
And my rhetoric too small
But the words in my verse
Are for one and for all

This is plebeian poetry
Simple sayings, simple rhymes
It's easy, you see
Taking little to no time

55. Nothing I Now Lack

I walk on the rail
Down through the woods
Following the trail
The feeling is good

Pen in my fingers
Pad at my side
The feeling still lingers
As the pen starts to glide

The wild facing before me
The road at my back
With God's Spirit He leads
There is nothing I lack

56. Take Flight

Take flight my companions
Like birds in the sky
Float like a phantom
As you pass the world by

Float past the trials
And the tribulations it holds
With a wink and a smile
When you do it be bold

We must cast all our cares
On this solid strong rock
With our hearts being laid bare
As one of his flock

57. The River

The river it flows
Out of our being inside
Its current never slows
And it's unaffected by tides

Consisting of living fluid
As odd as it seems
Its streams aren't diluted
With life it still teems

Of this Christ taught
In John chapter seven
It's for all who have sought
A way into Heaven

58. Antipsychotics

I can be terribly neurotic
With fears and obsessions
Thank God for antipsychotics
And for poetic expression

59. Unseen

Unseen but still felt
Like the blowing of wind
Within He has dwelt
Cleansing those who have sinned

His Spirit did rest
On Christ like a dove
When He began His first quest
Coming down from above

Like fire it consumes
Bringing power unto men
Hovering, He looms
Like chicks with their hen

60. My Soul You See

Into my soul You see
And into my person You peer
All I am or will be
My thoughts and my fears

You love me the same
On my darkest of days
This love You can't tame
There's no knowing its ways

Search me oh Lord
Try me and know
That as I move forward
Only with You will I go

61. He is King!

The Lord He is great
Never will He fail you
Though He gives and will take

The Lord He is strong
Breaking the bow and spear
He rejoices over you with a song

The Lord He is mighty
Ruling the nations with power
His reign is beyond sight

The Lord He is king!
Sitting enthroned above the flood
And covering you with His wings

62. My Love

My nurse in sickness
And clarity in the same
Wisdom when I'm witless
And coach in the game

You're there at my side
And there you remain
I would have lost heart or had died
If you didn't keep me sane

The journey has just begun
Our feet are on the bricks
There's much race left to be run
But with you, babe, I'll stick

63. To the Brim

No man knows tomorrow
Or who will survive
Will we have to beg or borrow
When that day does arrive?

No man's promised another
But there's still no excuse
To not be a keeper of your brother
Or let your passions run loose

We must live today
In honor of Him
Who has shown us the way
And fills our lives to the brim

64. Not Too Tall

I'm getting my act together
Trying to get on the ball
Thus far I've withstood the weather
Still standing but not too tall

65. We'll Shine!

Is there a calm around?
Is there a stillness above?
As His feet touch the ground
Met by those whom He loves

I think it will be fairly hectic
When the tribes see the sign
Perhaps this is too poetic
To say that they'll mourn but we'll shine!

66. When Your Head is a Mess

You'll never be on time
And never look your best
You'll be unable to rhyme
When your head is a mess

You won't be able to cope
You'll always be giving less
You'll feel like a dope
When your head is a mess

Pray to God enthroned
To keep your mind at its best
Peace is found in Him alone
When your head is a mess

67. What's Inside

Guide my hand
As these words I transcribe
Make them soft as sand
As I reveal what's inside

Direct my sayings
As they leave my tongue
Let them not sound like braying
But rather a song being sung

Instruct my ways and works
As I travel along
This burden I won't shirk
As I rhyme my silly song

68. Where Do You Stand?

Where do you stand
On this eternal decision
On which side of the land?
Remember, you can't make a revision

On one side is life
And the other side is death
On one side is strife
And it has no rest

The choice seems like a given
At least for me and others
Stand with the One who is risen
Stand with your sisters and brothers

69. This Burden We Now Bear

The ground began to shake
Just as He had said
As Christ began to wake
And He rose from the dead

The guards were stunned
And the women amazed
When they saw the Risen One
And at Him they all gazed

He told his disciples to go
And preach everywhere
This fact we surely know
And this burden we now bear

70. A New Page

A new beginning
And a new page
With hope I am singing
As I'm released from this cage

With You I will fly
Into fresh horizons
Passing troubles on by
As we shine like a diamond

My heart will no longer ache
With this knowledge I rejoice
As Your hand I humbly take
And I hear Your sweet voice

71. Welcome Home

The meadows and the lark
The snails and the thorns
The branches and the bark
And the dawn being born

This all was so costly
He thinks as He sits on His throne
And God whispers quite softly
Welcome home, son, welcome home

72. Face Adversity

In the shadows a man grows
In the dirt he matures
If you're caught in life's throws
Of these truths you'll be sure

A man must face adversity
And we are all called to suffer
So take pain in its diversity
For it's making you tougher

No one goes untouched
On this side of the ground
But His word we must clutch
If we wish to make it to the final round

73. Go Home

What can a young man do
To straighten his path?
Where should he move
To avoid sin's aftermath?

Should he remain
In filth with the swine?
Or should he sustain
His life back in the vine?

The man should go home!
For his father he waits
He'll meet his son who roams
Even before he reaches the gates

74. Given a Measure

The faith of a seed
Can produce a great deed

The faith of a mountain
Can make stone into a fountain

We're each given a measure
This was God's pleasure

Through faith we're redeemed
Though dead we had seemed

Through faith we're forgiven
And have this life that we're living

75. I'm Enmeshed

Bone of my bone
And flesh of my flesh
My person you now own
To you I'm enmeshed

All animals had a mate
But for man there was none
He was in a lonely state
Until something was done

God made Adam rest
And took from his side
And now men attest
With our wives we abide

76. To You I Was Faithful

This life is confusing
And how I do wonder
To God are we amusing
When we scream like the thunder?

How could this happen?
Your servant wails at the sky
In the cell that I'm trapped in
I cry and I cry

To You I was faithful
When the world turned its back
Toward sin I was hateful
Now why do I lack?

I know that You're holy
Enthroned in our praises
You look on the lowly
In all of our phases

To You I will look
When my back's against the wall
My name's in Your book
For to You I will call

77. God Surely Recalls

Do the righteous perish
Without God interceding?
Does He remember His cherished
And not answer their pleading?

God surely recalls
The righteous man's woes
Though it seemed He had stalled
His Spirit still flows

God will answer the man
Who calls on His name
It's in His will and plan
To rescue the same

78. On God's Holy Hill

Man shall eat their fill
And buy wine and milk
On God's holy hill

We'll all conform to His will
Being made like His Son
On God's holy hill

Each other's blood we won't spill
As we beat our spears into pruning hooks
On God's holy hill

Our passions we'll kill
As we're made new
On God's holy hill

Christ paid our bill
Now we can ascend
Onto God's holy hill

Now we wait until
Christ stands to the east
Of God's holy hill

79. The Rising of the Sun

This life is a pilgrimage
It is a process
To be conformed to His image

From glory to glory
And from day unto day
He's writing our story

Stand with the One
Who knows the end of the tale
And sets the rising of the sun

Be sure that He'll finish this work in you
Just as He feeds all the birds
He'll change you before life is through

80. Streams in the Desert

Like streams in the desert
And honey to the tongue
Your word is a treasure
That only just begun

Let it lead me into
All the ways You've ordained
As You carry me through
By You I am sustained

Let it tell me of things
That must be refined
Oh the joy that it brings
As my soul begins to align

81. The Victory You've Won

I will build the old waste places
Raising up the foundations of generations
This will be done in Your good graces
As You reconcile with the nations

I will repair the breach
And restore the streets to dwell in
Your law I will teach
To those who've turned from sin

Let their light break forth
As the shining of dawn
Let them see their true worth
And the victory You've won

82. Between My Blinking

They say time heals
But I can't help thinking
Am I just spinning my wheels
As life passes between my blinking?

Time makes some sour
Time can make some's wisdom profound
But it will all be devoured
When we return to the ground

I wonder about my demeanor
In the days when I'm old
Will my pride be much leaner
Or will I still be so bold?

Will I be one of the wise
Who sit at the gate
Or will I be despised?
Oh what is my fate?

83. Crisp in the Air

There's a crisp in the air
As the leaves begin to fall
The tan turns to fair
As the geese fly and make calls

The pumpkins are now here
Along with apple pie
The hunters chase the deer
And the bears start to hide

Families will soon gather
And sit with each other
We'll all start to blather
Cherishing time with our brothers

84. Sit and Wallow

Just let me sit and wallow
Like a pig in its filth
For my sins are too much to swallow

Why do I always return
Like a dog to its vomit?
This is my deepest concern

Why are men so weak
And bent on unrighteousness?
This is a sad condition of which I speak

Will a man seek right if he could?
We always choose the crooked
Man is incapable of good

85. My Being

These words express my being
The wells that are inside
They tell of the things I am feeling
The things that in me reside

These words bring emotions to life
And allow me to speak the unspoken
May they cut you like a knife
And leave your core bent and broken

These words do incarnate
My hidden deep parts
They make my passions awake
As I look into my heart

86. Old to Young

From old to young generations
We pass down our ways
The old becomes a new revelation
For the ones beginning their days

We are responsible to nurture
Our families into mature status
Growth is a part of our nature
Like vines crawling up a lattice

87. Sage

I wish to remember my vitality
And talk about it in my old age
But my grandkids will see my mortality
And question if I'm really a sage

88. Brother

With hearts knit together
And souls bound in like manner
I'll be with you, brother, wherever
My love will be your high banner

Our memories reflect each other
Like water facing a mirror
But I never needed a mirror, brother
To read your heart clearer

Next to you I wish to be laid beside
Six feet down in the earth
Just as in our mother we rested inside
During the time before our birth

89. Mornings

The mornings are still dark
The evenings are staying that way too
Fall seems to be making its mark
As frost replaces the dew

Let this season of decay behold
Bring with it a beauty to cherish
When the air starts to get cold
And when the foliage starts to perish

Soon the frost will turn to ice
And the rain will turn to snow
I know I won't have to tell you twice
That God's with you wherever the weather goes

90. A Word to the Wise

A word to the wise
And a word to the simple
Don't do long good-byes
But let your love be a symbol

Know that when two depart
They'll be reunited again
In person or in heart
Though there's no telling when

Carry him with you
Don't let her thought leave your mind
For you are one, no longer two
And your flesh God did bind

91. The Castle

The castle is made of strong stone
Its tower reaches high
A refuge for the alone
In the gaze of God's loving eye

Its gates are made of iron
Its bridge is made of bronze
Its ruled by the tribal lion
Within it you hear his songs

The king calls it his palace
And the prince his resting place
Come drink wine from the city's chalice
And of its wedding feast you must taste

92. This Heart of Mine

Take this heart of mine
I put it in your hands
As you give me thine
And we travel to different lands

My soul within me mourns
And my head begins to wilt
As from my hands you're torn
Our union must be rebuilt

93. The Storm

The storm is now back
And my stomach's uneasy
I'm under attack
I'm feeling too queasy

What do I do, Father
To reach the other side?
Should I even bother
To fight against the tide?

My heart now is broken
My head is in bits
Give me the Word you have spoken
To help with these psychotic fits

94. Save Me!

My feet now are numb
And the water is climbing up
I feel so dumb
Enough is enough

How could this happen
Right here and right now?
I feel I am strapped in
To a ship with a broken bow

Oh come and save me!
Like you have done in the past
Your servant you must see
I'm the least of the last

95. Stuck in the Sty

How can I beat this
And should I even try
All might be amiss
I'm stuck in the sty

How do I overcome
And beat my demons?
I look to the One
When my ground is uneven

Lord help me I plead!
Establish my feet
Your comfort I need
Before I'm sifted as wheat

96. Hole

I'm digging a hole
To bury myself in
This life takes a toll
With the places I've been

Someone come and tell me
That it'll be alright
Show me what I will be
And if I will win this long fight

97. The Door

Hopefully this helps you
And you can learn to empathize
In order to get through
I must learn to strategize

Maybe you can assist
And show me the way out
There's a lot of what I've missed
In fighting this deadly bout

There is a hope I'm sure
That will bring this to a close
At the end there is a door
But I know not where it goes

98. Cryptic Words

Cryptic words are spoken
That float in the air like leaves
They are symbols and a token
Of what my soul means

These emotions I let out
Through the medium of words
In them I express doubt
May they cut through like a sword

99. Puzzled

Deeply puzzled and puzzled still
How do I conform
To Your perfect will?

My heart going one way
My flesh to the other
But with You I wish to stay

Perhaps with some time
I'll learn to persist
In using my mind
To do as You insist

100. He Who

He who draws the line
For the waves in the sand
He who measures the oceans
In the hollow of His hands

He who makes darkness His hiding place
But lives in unapproachable light
He whose ways are beyond comprehension
And whose being is beyond sight

He who was slain before the world was
And who was killed on that tree
He who destroyed the power of Satan
Is He who lives within me

101. We Revolve

Like water under the bridge
Our history has floated away
And now standing on a ridge
We see our future in a new way

Our past hurts are forgiven
Our hang-ups have been resolved
We have a new world in which we live in
And around Christ's forgiveness we revolve

It is freeing to let go
And let the past be the past
There's less confusion and woe
For God's grace is unending and vast

102. My Sins

As far as the east is from the west
And into the depths of the sea
Now my soul can find rest
When you cast my sins far away from me

103. What a Mournful Song

Why is all such vanity?
And why a grasping for the wind?
How does the king retain his sanity
When he has to face his own sin?

Does it profit a man
If he gains the world's riches
But his soul can't withstand
And is left battered and in stiches?

Did he really gain anything
When he got the world's wealth?
What a mournful song he did sing
When he was old with failing health

104. I Will Stay

You have ordered my steps
And determined my way
On Your righteous path I have kept
And right by Your side I will stay

This road now is winding
With many turns and twists
But Your Word I am binding
And from Your side I won't shift

Down through the valley
And up on the mountain
Through the dark alley
Or in the torrent and fountain

You're wherever my feet touch
And wherever my soul travels
Despite the enemy's cruel clutch
And despite the road's grit and gravel

105. In a Blink

A grave mistake
That some may make

Is to think
Life doesn't pass in a blink

So before it's too late
Make sure you'll make it to the gates

106. The Skies

When I look to the skies
Your glory is revealed
In the darkness of night
This truth You have sealed

You stretch out the canopy
Like You're drawing out a curtain
Bold and bare all can see
Making Your power most certain

This creation is pure
Like a crystal clear river
Its light will endure
In the hands of the Giver

107. My Gem

My gem I almost lost
Because of my own foolishness
How great it would have cost
If I lost my love most luminous

Stay with me forever
And ever plus a day
Depart from me never
For without you life is so gray

I promise to try harder
And to open up much more
Before you I set a guard
With my heart behind a door

You see me fully now
Clear as the day breaks
My honesty I do vow
For both of our sakes

108. The Hour

No man knows the hour
Or the day in which He'll come
But darkness will be devoured
With the return of God's holy Son

You'll stand on the Mount of Olives
And split it right in two
On this mount You gave them knowledge
Now a river runs right through

From this day onward now
All creation no longer groans
All to You must bow
As You set up Your eternal throne

109. Celestial Air

Your house is for all nations
And it is a house of prayer
There they go and form relations
In the celestial air

Those from the east
And those from the west
Sit down to a feast
And all are called blessed

God calls all the tribes
He beckons all the tongues
Their names He inscribes
Both the old and the young

110. Like You

We'll look like You, Lord
And will be created anew
When our bodies are restored

No more sin and shame
No more death and decay
When You give us a new name

We know not yet what we shall be
But we'll sure live forever
In our glorified bodies

This toil and pain
Will all melt away
When You and I look the same

111. Dark Days

Here come the dark days
With much longer nights
It's the time when you just lay
In your bed and hide from the light

The temperature starts to drop
And we put on warm clothes
When the warm breeze stops
And the cold wind starts to blow

So, get some good friends
And stay somewhere cosy
Because the snow God will surely send
And our cheeks will get rosy

112. Within the Deep

How can we truly see
What lies within the deep?

Each man knows not himself
And within is a dark wealth

Only God can peer in
And look past all our sins

Oh what do You see
When You are looking at me?

What do You find,
Tell me, for I am so blind

113. The Wall

This wall has appeared
The wall which all souls find
The wall which I have feared
The wall that I can't climb

A wall which stops me cold
The wall which binds me still
The wall of which you're told
The wall within God's will

114. What Can We Do?

What can this beast do
To overcome his desires?
Which way does he move
To escape this cruel fire?

A man is the same
Always being ruled
And these passions we can't tame
We live on like pure fools

The power that lifts
This burden from our back
Is He who's given the gift
Of victory over evil's attack

115. My Soul's Hollows

The curse always follows
It creeps and it haunts
Within my soul's hollows
And my peace it does taunt

This black gift that's so bad
It takes and it steals
All the pleasure I would've had
My fate, it seems, has been sealed

Will I ever escape this?
This pit of despair
Will I again see bliss?
It's simply not fair

116. This New Body

This new body
Formed from many parts
Grafted and fitted together
Is like a work of art

We come from all around
The east, west, north and south
The earth will hear the sound
Of Your praise within our mouths

You've called us all out
From the kingdom of evil
With worship we'll shout
As we meet under Your steeple

117. The True End

We're almost done with this stretch
But no one knows the true end
Still we try to plan and sketch
And presumption is always the trend

We try to see God's thoughts
And these men say they all know
So we try and connect the dots
For what the Bible just doesn't show

118. All That We Do

We sing hallelujah to You
As You reign from your throne
We worship in all that we do
To make Your name known

We praise You for Your grace
And for Your holiness as well
We long to see Your face
And with You eternally dwell

You oh Lord are King
And judge of all us men
Creator of everything
But You call me Your own friend

119. Creation

All creation waits
And right now is groaning
Oh what will be the date
When it ceases its moaning

God made a promise
To renew and restore
Our failings that look like Thomas's
And the seas and its shore

Terrance John Cummins

120. This Burden You're Hauling

He rescues us from our fall
And their consequences too
This burden you're hauling
He takes it with you

One day all will be tried
The fire will burn hot
Good works will be purified
And our failings will not

121. Life Is Like a Road

Life is like a road
That was built upon a trail
That somehow got sold
And the Devil made the sale

What was once beautiful and lush
Is now broad and packed
The foliage which we'd touch
Is something now that we lack

Life started in the garden
All those years ago
But now we seek a pardon
Once our sins had been sown

122. When I Am Gone

Forget me not
When I pass on
Visit my plot
When I am gone

Remember the good
The times when we laughed
When they lower the wood
And send down my floating raft

When all that's left
Are some bones and a stone
My love you'll have kept
When I'm in my new home

123. Like a Stain

Will I bring change
To this craft that I admire?
I want to be within range
Of taking it much higher

But my words are so plain
So bent and so broken
They're on this page like a stain
Truer words haven't been spoken

124. Your Purpose

Your purpose is hidden
Like a treasure in a field
But it's not forbidden
It'll soon be revealed

You'll see it as you walk
Down the path God has ordained
Of its grandeur you'll talk
And its form you'll ascertain

So keep your eyes peeled
As we move heaven bound
Your purpose is now sealed
It's buried underground

125. A Song on My Lips

With a joy filled heart
And a song on my lips
I know you won't depart
Our love you'll never quit

Though an ocean was between
And a great gulf was fixed
My love went unseen
But was always in your midst

And now we stand together
With each other in our arms
To you my soul is tethered
And by you it is charmed

126. This Wood

This wood You have made
Became the handle for the blade

And this created rock
Was shaped into a stock

That same tree
You carried for me

And those were my nails
But no one paid Your bail

As they put thorns within Your head
You soon would fall dead

In a tomb You were laid
And for three days there You stayed

But new life You'd see
And in rising You'd set us free

Terrance John Cummins

127. Christ Dwells Inside

Now that Christ dwells on the inside
Even though my flesh may tire
Within me He'll abide
This mortal He'll make alive
And instill His own desires
Now that Christ dwells inside
My passions have been revived
And my sin I will retire
Within me He'll abide
Regardless of the tide
He'll pull me from the mire
Now that Christ dwells inside
This truth in me now resides
Ever taking me higher
Within me He'll abide
This life I now take in stride
And I am filled with fresh fire
Now that Christ dwells inside
Within me He'll abide

128. Zion

These hands that are marred
And this heart that is charred
How can they ascend Your hill?
If I'm failing to conform to Your will

My hands show their scars
And this heart is set in bars
How can I enter if I'm still unclean?
I can't, it would seem

But there is one of whom I've heard
Who washes with His pure Word
My heart He can mend
And Zion I will now ascend!

129. Blind Leaders

Exceedingly above my thoughts
And soaring higher than my ways
This wisdom the world sought
But in foolishness we have stayed

The Rock of the Ages
The wisest of all
Confounds the soundest sages
Both the big and the small

His understanding lives on
And none can fathom His mind
From which we've feebly drawn
We're just blind leaders of the blind

130. Winter

The sound of the crow
And the settling of the snow
Tell when winter has come
And when summer is all done

I pray that it is short
So to poetry I resort
Looking for warm memories
To which I will flee

131. This Man

Oh this Man we write
Who changed us all for good
Who makes burdens light
And sacrificed all that He could

This man we now preach
Who became one of us
To show God is within reach
Him we could finally touch

Listen to what we say
That Christ became a slave
On the world's darkest day
It was His life that He gave

But on the third day He arose
And ascended into Heaven
After serving so low
He purges us from all leaven

132. For Me

It was for me that He came
The beggar and the thief
Bearing all our shame
And bringing our relief

Our cross He did bear
And He took all our nails
His flesh they did tear
Leaving Him dead and pale

This He did to atone
For the sin that I'd commit
He gave me a new home
And my name He now won't omit

133. The Heart

The heart is very deceitful
And wicked above all else
It rages like a bull
Thinking only of itself

Out of its abundance we speak
And you'll keep it with your treasure
Sadly, its just so weak
And chases after pleasure

Out of it flows our lives
We must keep it guarded
Along our dreadful plights
Or from God's peace we will have parted

134. The Day I Called

You drew near on the day I called
And lifted me out of the hole
Though the enemy left me mauled
And all my pleasure he had stole

It is good for me to bear
This yoke now in my youth
Carrying it with me You share
And teach me this painful truth

I know the sun will rise
And the rains they shall cease
I'll soon stop believing these lies
And start treasuring my peace

135. Toward Him

The Great designer
Has a yearning
For the cursory and minor
Toward Him they are turning

The crooked and the vile
Float into your arms
Though they leave a taste like bile
And have done some serious harm

The Lord forgives fully
And doesn't turn them away
Leave you? Never would he.
But with you He'll ever stay

136. Pureness

He splits the seas
And makes a fountain from stone
From Him the heavens flee
And all creation groans

He created it all
With the breath of His mouth
He brought judgment to our fall
And is supreme with all clout

The horse and the rider
He has thrown into the depths
Its saddle and bridle
Under the waters were swept

He was in the furnace
And there at the flood
Serve the Lord with pureness
Because for you He shed his blood

137. His Voice

The roar of the lion
And the bleating of the lamb
The sound of many waters
As they crash onto the sand

How can we hear
The sound of His voice
It cuts through like a spear
But it's still a beautiful noise

His echo breaks the cedars
And strips the forest bare
They speak to their reader
As they float on through the air

138. Broken Legs

My knees are weak
And the ground feels like it quakes
These words I can't speak
As the floor starts to break

My mind now is falling
As I trip down the stairs
My growth now is stalling
And I'm growing gray hairs

Having a beaten mind
Is like walking with broken legs
There's no peace you can find
You're left only the dregs

139. The King

With Your iron sceptre
With Your eyes of fire
You float like a spectre
And all will call You sire

Your face it clearly shines
In brilliance like the sun
It fires and is refined
Like a nickel-plated gun

The hair of Your head
Was white and glowing
John felt dead
Because Your glory You were showing

140. You Must Quell

Though God may surely test
He certainly won't tempt
But the unwanted guest
Rest assured he will make an attempt

He'll offer you an inch
And end up taking you a mile
And when he prepares your lynch
He'll be cracking a crooked smile

That snake from below
The angel that fell
Put him in his hole
And his rebellion you must quell

141. My Craft

To make you laugh
And to make you merry
Is my sincere craft
Just to keep it light and airy

My demeanour may seem serious
And my brow far too furrowed
But my humor isn't mysterious
And my laughter won't be burrowed

Laughter makes you healthy
And makes life worthwhile
It may not make you wealthy
But it will take you miles and miles

142. An Irishman

I've got all the signs
With the map on my face
Mental illness of all kinds
But my being I embrace

My love for a good story shows
And my pleasure to write would indicate
I'm an Irishman of many woes
But my many sins Christ does vindicate

143. His Spirit

It's power for the meek
Above the waves of today
It's knowledge to seek
His most unsearchable ways

Christ gives you this gift
And on you He bestows
His will that He might lift
You out of sin's bitter throws

His Spirit lives within
And emboldens you here and now
Giving you victory over sin
Of this He does vow

144. Tough Times Don't End Overnight

It's like gasping for air
And trying to stay above the waves
The heroes felt this and did share
When they wandered in dens and caves

They faced death and trouble
They saw persecution and shame
Being reduced to stubble
And their followers saw the same

So sorry for the mournful song
It's because tough times don't end overnight
They endure throughout and are long
And a lot of times it's going to be a fight

145. How I Wish To Live

With ease and levity
Is how I wish to live
It'll give me some longevity
And I'll always look to forgive

But this is just a dream
A fantasy in my head
For it would certainly seem
That to burdens I am wed

I feel them when I wake
And when I lay down again
But a man they're beginning to make
I see it every now and then

146. My Way

Make my way straight
Straighter than an arrow
And as for the gate
Make it very narrow

I'll avoid the path that is broad
And the gate that is crooked
The world I'll never laud
Although it appears so lurid

147. Graces

Can we forgive the one who hurt
And overlook his trespass?
Or should we just be curt
And admit our graces won't last?

Remember it was you
Who sinned against the King
And He forgave you too
Of every single thing

Also, don't you forget
That it certainly is freeing
To forgive your brother's debt
It sanctifies your being

148. My Heart

My heart you have stolen
It's heavy with love
In your hand it is swollen
And dripping on your gloves

In my chest there is a cavity
Where this organ once was
My words they have gravity
I'm not saying them just because

Treat it with care
And love me back sincerely
I'll never leave you I swear
And I'll treat you very dearly

149. My Struggles

My struggles aren't hidden
In fact, everyone now knows
Because of them I have written
Of both the highs and the lows

Hopefully these struggles of mine
Can help you along your way
It's fine to not be fine
And it's okay to not be okay

150. Cloudy

Do I need some glasses?
Because I'm seeing badly
I'm not like the masses
Because I think so madly

This paranoia clouds my vision
And taints how I see the world
I fear that its causing division
As reality and fantasy are swirled

Hopefully this won't last forever
Although I'm not setting high hopes
My peace has long been severed
But for peace I still grasp and grope

151. Fix Every Part

I have open hands
And a humble heart
Mend me with bands
And fix every part

I have nothing without you
Except tribulation and loss
And there's nothing I can do
To get out of this chaos

From where does my help come?
As I look to the hills
When I am beaten as a drum
I'll just know and be still

152. The End

Follow the flow with its bends
And you'll soon find the way
But this seems like our end
At least for today

153. A Friend Once Said

Take care of your soul
A friend once said
And seek to control
The thoughts in your head

Because thoughts turn into words
And words turn into deeds
So may they lift you like a bird
And carry you like a steed

This may seem like a daydream
If peace you have never held
But know that with hope God's promise teems
For the one who with God truly melds

154. For All

For fools and for sages
For the weak and the strong
For the poor and those who pay wages
For the right and the wrong

For the young and the old
For the black and the white
For the shy and the bold
And be it day or night

This message is for all
And its truth for everyone
So may you answer the call
Before your time is done

155. God's Home

With eagerness we arrive
In God's holy town
No longer to strive
As we take our new crowns

There will no longer be loss
And toil or pain
Great was the cost
That bought us this gain

Forever we'll remember
The price that He paid
When death puts out our embers
And when our bodies are remade

156. The River

The river it surges
And with it comes debris
Our peace it purges
As we try to flee

How do we contain this
And how are we to sleep
When our journeying is aimless
And the road is too steep?

It's hard to win the battle
That's fought between your ears
But this bull you'll learn to straddle
As you ride it through your years

Terrance John Cummins

157. Pain

A sad man once said
To a man to whom he was led

"How can you be so glad
When with pain this world is clad?"

Despite his aggression
The man returned his question

"For your pain there is a reason
And it'll endure for but a season"

The sad man carried on
Singing his somber song

But eventually he did realize
As he looked upon the skies

These times in which we're tested
And the pain we had protested

All work together for the good
And even Christ had to carry His wood

158. Beyond Us

Go take a walk
To the edge of the earth
Listen to how the waves talk
And get caught up in their surf

Look up above
And peer down below
See the intricacies thereof
And the complexities they show

This creation is beyond us
And far past our comprehension
How could we discuss
This that captures our attention?

159. Bands of Love

The earth is the Lord's
And the fullness thereof
He draws us with cords
And with bands of love

The Lord made it all
All creation and its splendour
But only man's burdens He hauls
And with us He is tender

What is man?
That You are mindful of him
And how great is Your plan
To redeem us of sin!

160. How Can Man Know?

How can man know
What stands behind the turn?
Something that makes us grow
Or something that we'll learn?

Our paths may be hidden
And our journey mysterious
But this far we have ridden
And to turn back would be serious

So keep on moving
And riding your horse
Not knowing what God is doing
Means you're on the right course

161. Be Vigilant

A folding of the hands
And a little bit of sleep
Can bring the end of a man
For destruction it creeps

Keep your eyes peeled
For your enemy roams about
His tricks are now revealed
And his roaring is loud

He seeks to devour
The man who is unaware
And the earth he does scour
So be vigilant in prayer

162. The Heavens

The Heavens rotate
And bring with them new stars
As we stand at the celestial gate
We see Venus and Mars

The heavens do declare
The Glory of God
How do we compare
Since we are made of earth's sod?

But of us You are mindful
And You care for our sorrows
Even though we are prideful
You still hold our tomorrows

163. Not Forgotten Lore

The train of his robe
Covers the temple floor
He's known throughout the globe
It's not just forgotten lore

The earth is His footstool
And heaven is His throne
Endless is His rule
And His faithfulness is known

Is there any god like Him?
Are there any who can save?
Without Him life is grim
And its end is the grave

164. Like Fire

Like fire under dry brush
And sun on dried skin
My anger leaves me crushed
And my piety just can't win

Raging through the day
And turning through the night
I can't find the way
For my peace is out of sight

Is it wrong to be mad
And to clench your fists?
For one, I'm sure it's bad
To keep throwing raging fits.

165. A Man Should Trust

Under Your shadow I'll be found
And within Your tower I will live
I'll be safe and sound
With this life that You give

A man should trust Him
You should trust in God's plan
Don't plot yours on a whim
This is done by a foolish man

He guides those in his shadow
And leads those in his tower
Out of the depths and into the shallow
He helps them in their worst hour

166. Proceed

It's okay to be tired
And it's alright to be exhausted
When you don't get what's desired
Or when you're being accosted

Sometimes we all feel like quitting
And giving up on going on
When we're practice for hitting
And used as a pawn

But you've come so far already
So quitting isn't an option
Keep moving forward and steady
And proceed without caution

167. Distractions

A sign of our times
Is seen in our actions
We ignore the sublime
And are engrossed in distractions

Our knowledge is increasing
As people run to and fro
But our humanity is ceasing
And our compassions are low

To keep our way pure
And to make it more straight
We must look for a cure
Before it's too late

168. The Woman

The woman with the problem
This issue of blood
She touched Christ's hem's bottom
As she crawled in the mud

Power had left Him
As He turned around
But He didn't see when He skimmed
This woman on the ground

"Who is it that touched Me?
For I know power has left"
Finally, He did see
And up to Him she had crept

"It was I who had touched
The hem of your cloak
Your fabric I clutched
And this curse you have broke"

"Be of good cheer!
Your faith has made you well
My message is clear
And of these deeds you will tell!"

169. Water

A river may overflow
And it may twist like a snake
But to the ocean it goes
Or on into a lake

Our life is like the river
Flowing on downstream
Whichever way it slivers
There's always something to glean

The journey is meant to grow
Although some of it is hard
If the river is fast or slow
There's still nothing we should discard

170. Treasure

A timeless treasure
Is love in a young couple
These two seek pleasure
And their expressions aren't subtle

A man should enjoy
The wife of his youth
His pain she'll destroy
For his stress she will sooth

Savor it now!
And hold it so dear
When your love is at the bow
And not at the rear

Terrance John Cummins

171. These Poems

The poems that I write
Are airy and light

The words that I pen
Soar every now and again

They're silly and short
And my meaning they distort

For behind these two eyes
And behind all these lies

Stand the truth of our being
And our light that is gleaming

But it's so hard to express!
And I usually just make a mess

172. The Power of His Might

Isaiah and Jeremiah write
While David and Solomon sing
The power of His might
And the beauties of the King

Of Him Zechariah spoke
And of Him Jacob prophesied
That day when Christ awoke
Was written by the scribe

It's all in this book
And found in this scroll
Go and take a look
It'll refresh your soul

173. Double Mind

A man with a double mind
Is like the waves of the shore
He'll have confusion of all kinds
And he'll never be quite sure

He'll be unstable in all his ways
Tossed to and fro and all about
Like the crashing of waves
Unless he begins to re-route

Fix your mind on things above
And let it be renewed
Meditate on God's love
Before you become unglued

174. Noah

The men began to turn
And all their thoughts were evil
God decided to destroy but not burn
All of the Earth's people

But there was a man spared
And his family with him too
Who escaped the snare
Because the ark brought them through

The rains began to fall
And the earth began to flood
To all the animals Noah called
For he was perfect in blood

When the water began to recede
And the raven was sent out of the window
The dove brought back a branch from a tree
For the waters had gotten low

They left the ark
When it rested on the mount
The flood left its mark
And all the animals they had to count

God then made a promise
And set his rainbow in the sky
Noah sacrificed and showed homage
But got drunk before he died

175. A Time

A time to sleep
And a time to wake
A time to weep
For our sorrow's sake

A time to throw
And a time to gather
A time to grow
In the things that matter

A season to recall
All the songs that we've sung
God wants this season for all
Who have been born under the sun

176. A Choice

A choice is before us
To choose life or death
To be sinful or just
Or greater or less

In whom do you trust?
Which way do you choose?
Before you return to dust
And you've paid your final dues

The two thieves next to Christ
One said "yes" the other "no"
The wise one chose life
While the other was sent below

177. Take Root

Let this word take root
And you'll grow like a tree
You'll eat of its fruit
And God's glory you'll see

The word is a seed
That grows on the inside
It challenges your deeds
But in it you'll confide

These words are a gift
They help me live and learn
Like the crafting of a smith
Towards them I'll turn

178. The Tongue

The speaking of a word
Can bring life if you hear
Or the hurt it incurs
Makes life seem less dear

The power of the tongue
Can make you taste death
Like men when they're hanged
Or have been shot through the chest

The results are up to you
Will you choose growth or decay?
Make them pleasant or true?
And in God's blessing you'll stay

179. By the Rivers That Flowed

These hands they have labored
And this brow it has sweat
Freedom we now savor
But in Babylon we wept

We had hung our harps
By the rivers that flowed
And then we embarked
On the long journey home

Zerubbabel has started the work
His hands shall also finish
Though the enemy still lurks
This temple won't diminish

Terrance John Cummins

180. John

A prisoner he sits
On an island far off
He's left in this pit
Because Christ he had sought

Patmos is isolated
Empty and a prison
So long he has waited
For Christ who is risen

All the others have died
And only John now is left
But Christ with blazing eyes
Appeared on a Sabbath Day's rest

He gave him a message
Then John saw many visions
Of beauty and wreckage
Of unions and divisions

John saw the close
And the new beginning
The story how it goes
Has evil losing and good winning

181. A Temper

A temper in a man
Can bring strife and trouble
A temper in a woman
Can be much more subtle

One who controls his emotions
And who guards his passions
Can get past the notion
That they must move with severe actions

The man who is stronger
Is he who controls his temper
His life will be longer
And he won't die out like embers

182. The Music

A song and a dance
Makes my heart merry
A tune and a prance
Lifts me as a fairy

The music it moves
From the strings to my ear
I shake and I groove
My love for it is dear

I hope when I am old
That songs are still there
I'll dance and be bold
When my hair is white and fair

183. Heavy

In this life that we're slaving
I've had my full fill
All this pain that we're saving
It leaves me bound and still

In this war that we're waging
My teeth will be gritted
And my face will be staging
But my fears won't be admitted

This life is so heavy
And these emotions take a toll
Even if you're not ready
It's coming for your soul

184. Written in His Journal

Come and go with me
Come take my hand
When you go you'll see
And in eternity you'll stand

You'll see streets of gold
And the river with life it teems
Enter the throne room being bold
It's the place of our dreams

This home will be eternal
But for now your days are on Earth
They're all written in his journal
Inscribed in poetic verse

185. Like Clay

Oh that my words were written
And engraved forever in stone
By them all would be smitten
And it would pierce even their bones

These words carry weight
And burn like a fire
They talk about my fate
And tell of the scars I've acquired

I try to mold them like clay
And carve them like wood
But eventually in the ground they'll lay
Because the test of time that wouldn't have withstood

186. Cement

What's in your heart
And what's in your soul
Is it gracefully like art
Or black as soot and coal

They say your heart is deceitful
And that it lays with your treasures
To break it would be lethal
And its depths we could never measure

God, I give this to you
My heart be it crooked and bent
Because my love for you grew
And my faith is starting to cement

187. Things in Heaven

What do you know
Of things in heaven
Things on earth
And things below

What have you been shown
Of things in heaven
Things on earth
And things below

I would let your wisdom grow
Of things in heaven
Things on earth
And things below

188. Hell

A cloud covers overhead
And fire is beneath
We walk among the dead
In the land of gnashing of teeth

Ruled by an angel of light
And 1/3 of the heavenly host
When they fell from that great height
To where the wicked eternally roast

Oh! What a place of torment
A place of shame and weeping
They'll never climb Abraham's ascent
Across this gulf there is no leaping

Where is the rest for him
Who finds himself in this pit?
As man is torn limb from limb
Finding no peace for his spirit

189. The Lamp of Your Body

The lamp of your body
Are the eyes in your head
So keep your peering godly
And you'll escape all the dread

If your eye be full of light
Your body will likely follow
But if it is dark as night
You'll be full of sorrow

This is what the Messiah said
In Matthew chapter six
This truth He did spread
And my perspective it has fixed

190. Ireland

My family, they all come
From the Emerald Isle
Where we cry until we're numb
And then fake all our smiles

The land covered by a cloud
Its so mystic and green
The land's been thoroughly ploughed
And for miles rock walls are seen

It's the home of the saints
The scholars and sages
Its writers they paint
The greatest tales of all ages

Though I'm across the waters
From that rock in the sea
It's the home of my fathers
And it lives on in me

Terrance John Cummins

191. The King on His Throne

Would you trust
The king on His throne
You certainly must
And only in Him alone
He knows your past
Your future and present
He knows what will last
And in what you'll be content

So even though the road is winding
Knowing not what's behind the curve
His blessing you'll be finding
If His instructions you observe

192. A Robe Dipped in Blood

A head with many crowns
And a robe dipped in blood
He watched them all drown
When He sat enthroned in the flood

Riding on a horse
With a title on His thigh
He sets judgment on its course
While He dwells on high

A sword in His mouth
And fire in His eyes
Sinners He casts out
You can still hear their cries

193. Our Bodies

The glory of the temple
The majesty of the crown
Within this earthen vessel
Is seen in its hidden renown

These bodies that He made
Out of dust and out of clay
His glory he has inlaid
And puts it on display

They one day will reflect
The image of Him
And you can surely expect
Its glory not to dim

194. Wrestle

The kingdom suffers violence
And the violent take it by force
This war brings no silence
As we travel along its course

Our weapons aren't carnal
But spiritual, taking strongholds
In this truth we do marvel
So we just do as we are told

Make yourself a vessel
For God to use in this fight
For with principalities we wrestle
On into the night

195. My Soul Ever Goes

The Israelites died in the desert
And didn't enter in the land
Their souls never touched the dirt
And from it they were banned

There remains therefore a rest
For the people who are true
Once they've completed the test
And their troubles are through

Waiting on the other side
Is a peace no mortal knows
Because only in the divine it abides
But toward it my soul ever goes

196. We Are All in Need

A man once did bellow
As he walked by my side
"If you ever meet a mean fellow
Don't just bicker and chide"

He continued as we carried on
Down the side of the road
"Because when you are gone
Your kindness won't leave him cold"

Finally he did finish
As we reached our destination
"Don't let your love for the cruel diminish
For we are all in need of salvation"

197. Anxiety, Depression, Paranoia

Anxiety is like a knife
Cutting through your brain
It has you mourn life
And question if you are sane

Depression is like a storm
Raging in the depths of night
It gathers all that's forlorn
And buries any hope of light

Paranoia curses my head
Seeing things not as they really are
Praying for peace but instead
Knowing its not near but very far

198. True Power

The power of a man
Isn't seen in his brawn
Or where his feet do stand
When his foes are dead and gone

No, true power lies
Deep within the heart
For the man whose sin dies
When his desires are torn apart

A man who learns to control
His actions, words, and thoughts
Is he who guards his soul
And wins the battle that is fought

Terrance John Cummins

199. The Burden

The burden of the world
Doesn't rest on you
It rests on the one
Who is faithful through and through

The weight of all its troubles
Isn't yours to bear
But this is so hard to see
When you count all your cares

200. Tribulation

A time is soon coming
When trials will sweep the Earth
Sounds of war will be drumming
When Zion travails in birth

The time of Jacob's trouble
Before the triumphant return
When the earth is reduced to rubble
And all creation burns

This is the time of tribulation
That's waiting at our door
So pray that your salvation
Is true at its very core

201. Oh That You Would Rend the Heavens

To You the heavens bow
And all the mountains smoke
Your glory fills the Earth now
With the fire that You stoked

As fire burns brushwood
And it causes water to boil
Make them know Your name is good
When You return upon Earth's soil

Oh, that You would come down!
That the mountains might tremble
All the people would hear the sound
And before You the nations would assemble

202. John 4

There by the well
Sat a thirsty man
Of His salvation He would tell
When He met the Samaritan

"Why do you speak to me?
For we and Jews and have no dealings"
She thought could this really be
He who has done all those healings

He said, "If you had only known
This man who you're seeing
Then waters would have grown
Out of your inmost being"

This prophet then spoke
Telling her all these things
And her soul within her awoke
And this message she began to bring

203. Fruit

The season of fruit
Has come to our fields
The crops with their dew
Have started to yield

The season of pruning
Is over and gone
The branches that were ruining
Have left with the dawn

The season of harvest
Has finally come
But there's no time to rest
When there's work to be done

204. Asleep in the Ship

A ship in the sea
Tossed to and fro
The Messiah's asleep
For His destiny He did know

He knew that this storm
Wasn't His end
For the cross He was born
To this He was sent

So don't you panic
If He's asleep in the ship
Although all seems frantic
You're still in His grip

205. We Embark

A time and a season
For all under the skies
For its all there for a reason
In our hopes and our sighs

The troubles and pains
The light and the dark
The sun and the rains
On this quest we embark

To find the purpose
For the sorrows in life
Though it leaves us wordless
And cuts like a knife

206. Right from the Start

From God don't depart
But with Him do stay
Right from the start
To the closing of day

For He'll never leave you
From your side He won't move
In all that you do
And whatever you choose

He's the friend that sits closer
Than even a brother
He'll hold your composure
Better than any other

207. A Life That's Pure

To pursue the cause
Of those in the noose
To make all pause
And listen to truth

To protect the weak
And encourage the poor
To truly be meek
And live a life that's pure

To feed the famished
And give drink to the thirsty
To give a home to the banished
Is showing God's mercy

208. The Sand is Running Low

Today is the day
And right now is the time
For you might have to pay
Before I finish this rhyme

Salvation is at the door
And stands waiting at the gate
May you desire it more
Before it's too late

The clock it is ticking
As the trumpet starts to blow
The hour glass is trickling
And the sand is running low

209. No One Who Could See

A tempest inside
And a calm without
To You I had cried
When I was stuck in the drought

I had no one to turn to
And no one who could see
That within the man that they knew
My mind was collapsing within me

You saw my frame
And knew I was just dust
I truly wasn't the same
But in You I could trust

Whenever I'm attacked
And whenever I am torn
You mend all my cracks
And calm every storm

210. Cold

Cold to my toes
And frozen to bits
The temp is so low
I'm losing my wits

Clouds leave my mouth
And my nose starts to freeze
I'm moving down south
To feel a warm breeze

211. Break Ups

The earth has its seasons
And the ocean has its tides
A man has his reasons
To say his goodbyes

It may be painful
And it'll last a few weeks
But its fruit is gainful
Although you'll have to start to seek

Break ups are an opportunity
To assess your actions
See what caused disunity
And what brought the factions

212. The Common

Blessed are the meek
The reviled and forgotten
So turn the other cheek
And live with the outcast and common

This feast was for the rich
But was given to the poor
God made the switch
When the rich closed their door

This kingdom is for us
The lost under these skies
The sinner made just
Towards heaven we'll rise

Terrance John Cummins

213. The Beating in My Chest

Dreams take form
When the clouds part
There's peace in the storm
And stillness in my heart

I'm beginning to hear again
That isle calling out to me
But I know not when
I will again cross those seas

That emerald in the waves
The jewel of the west!
To You I am enslaved
Yours is the beating in my chest

214. Emerald

My soul longs
For far distant shores
To hear their merry songs
And be greeted at their door

In that land that's an Emerald
I wish to lay my head
And be gently lulled
As I lay down in my bed

I wish to work and rest
On the isle that consumes me
But will I finish the test
Of helping them be set free?

I know that I was born
To help the Celts who are in pain
To complete this I have sworn
Because I carry with me God's name

215. My Will I Must Kill

Will I make it back
To the country of hills and walls
To where I was attacked
Will I answer this call?

Or will I stay here
With my friends and family
Where I enjoy health and cheer
But still carry this burden within me

I'll go back there!
One day I know I will!
For Ireland's sorrows I bear
But first my will I must kill

216. The Flesh

This flesh that we wrestle
Both night and day
The substance of the earthen vessel
Is only but dirt and clay

From dust we are made
And to dust we shall return
When in the ground we are laid
On to glory or to burn

One day this flesh will die
When we take our last breath
In that grave we will lie
Onward to heaven or the depths

217. Your Cross

Bring it to the altar
As you carry your cross
It's written in the psalter
That we'll pay the highest cost

Your life is an offering
And You are a living sacrifice
This story God is authoring
As we pay the highest price

This truth is now unsealed
Our deeds He will recount
And our words He will reveal
When we pay the greatest amount

218. Sloppy With Slurs

Short and in tempo
Sloppy with slurs
These words don't seem to glow
But hopefully they'll endure

This ink as the expression
My head as the source
It helps me in digressions
When I get way off course

Poetry's job is to explain
The thoughts in my head
My joys and my pains
And the things that go unsaid

219. A Carving of Words

A carving of words
A painting of phrases
This message we've heard
Passed down through the ages

That God gave his Son
And his Son gave His life
Its light has begun
To infiltrate the night

Take these words with you
Carry them day by day
Their truth will bring you through
And they're for all who have gone astray

220. A Writer

A year's gone by
And things have gotten better
I let out a gleeful sigh
Because I'm throwing off my fetters

These days have past
And so much has changed
Good memories I've amassed
And in my heart they'll be arranged

Everyday isn't flawless
But they certainly are brighter
For in Christ I find solace
And I'm turning back into a writer

Afterword

I wrote the majority of the poetry during September-October of 2018. I had been listening to a teaching on Hebrew poetry during my commute and it sparked something in me to start writing poetry again. Most of the writing I would either do when I had some free time at home, before work, or when my students had seat work or were at recess. This was at the point in my journey when I was home from Ireland after my second trip there. I had been home for about 10 months and had been recovering from mental illness. I had done some poetry writing in high school but hadn't done much in recent years. It was a ton of fun and I look forward to writing more in the future.

Printed in the United States
By Bookmasters